"Taking lessons from Jack Prelutsky, Kenn Nesbitt feeds kids a seemingly boundless feast of belly laughs and funny-bone ticklers."

"After sharing the CD, students clamored to the poetry section of the library to check out additional copies to use in Poetry Break performances...Teachers using this title to launch a poetry unit should plan on having several copies available for students to check out."

The Tighty Whitey Spider

The Tighty Whitey Spider

And More Wacky Animal Poems i Totally Made Up

Kenn Nesbitt

illustrated by Ethan Long

sourcebooks
jabberwocky

Copyright © 2010 by Kenn Nesbitt
Cover and internal design © 2010 by Sourcebooks, Inc.
Cover and internal illustrations by Ethan Long

Sourcebooks and the colophon are registered trademarks of
Sourcebooks, Inc.

Published by Sourcebooks Jabberwocky, an imprint of Sourcebooks, Inc.
P.O. Box 4410, Naperville, Illinois 60567-4410
(630) 961-3900
Fax: (630) 961-2168
www.jabberwockykids.com

Library of Congress Cataloging-in-Publication data is on file with the publisher.

Source of Production: Versa Press, East Peoria, Illinois, USA
Date of Production: April 2010
Run Number: 12100

Printed and bound in the United States of America
VP 10 9 8 7 6 5 4 3 2 1

For Kaylen and Dylan

Contents

POEM TITLE	PAGE	TRACK

Hear the author read (and sing!) some of his best-loved poems. (And even crack a few jokes!)

Download the free audio tracks here:
www.sourcebooks.com/extras/tighty-whitey-spider.html

Track List

THE TIGHTY WHITEY SPIDER

(to the tune of "The Itsy Bitsy Spider")

The tighty whitey spider went down the water slide.
Got a water wedgie halfway down the ride.
Jumped up and screamed and ran around in pain.
Now the tighty whitey spider will not do that again.

MY DOG PLAYS INVISIBLE FRISBEE

My dog plays invisible Frisbee.
He catches invisible balls.
He rides an invisible skateboard.
He hurdles invisible walls.

My dog has perfected the practice
of doing invisible tricks.
He jumps with invisible jump ropes
and fetches invisible sticks.

He barks at invisible mailmen.
He growls at invisible cats.
He'll bring me invisible slippers
and even invisible hats.

He chases invisible squirrels
whenever we go for a jog.
He's clearly the greatest dog ever.
I love my invisible dog.

MY KITTEN WON'T STOP TALKING

My kitten won't stop talking.
She just prattles night and day.
She walks around repeating
nearly everything I say.

My kitten never says, "Meow."
She never even purrs.
She mimics me instead
in that annoying voice of hers.

She waits for me to speak,
and then she copies every word,
or begs me for a cracker,
or says, "I'm a pretty bird."

I'm not sure what to do, and so
I simply grin and bear it.
She's been this way since yesterday;
that's when she ate my parrot.

MOLLY HAS A MYNA BiRD

Molly has a myna bird,
a raven, and a wren.
She loves her owl, her guinea fowl,
her hornbill, and her hen.

She keeps a crow, a condor,
and a cuckoo in her house.
An ostrich, hawk, macaw, and auk,
a grackle, and a grouse.

4

Her pets include a pelican,
a penguin, and a duck.
She thinks it's cute the way they hoot
and chirp and quack and cluck.

She's happy with her hummingbird,
her swift, and swallow too.
It's safe to say that only they
and nothing else will do.

You see, she has no hamster,
and she doesn't have a dog.
No snake, no rat, no tabby cat,
no ferret, fish, or frog.

She's never said she hates those pets
in quite so many words.
And yet you'll find, to Molly's mind,
they're strictly for the birds.

MY KiWi iS THE CAPTAiN

My kiwi is the captain of a supersonic plane
that doesn't fly to Switzerland or Singapore or Spain.
It doesn't fly to Jordan or Jamaica or Japan,
or Serbia, Somalia, Samoa, or Sudan.

It doesn't fly to Norway, Nicaragua, or Nepal.
It's safe to say it doesn't fly to anywhere at all.
But that's the way it always goes for kiwis, as you've heard.
It's true that he's a pilot, but he's still a flightless bird.

FROG BALL

In summertime and through the fall,
whenever frogs are playing ball,
it's normally a boring show.
For frogs do not know how to throw
or bat or steal or slide or run,
which means their games are never fun.

Instead, they simply sit around
the outfield and the pitcher's mound
and hope that someone hits the ball
and sends it sailing toward the wall.
For this should come as no surprise:
They're excellent at catching flies.

i BOUGHT OUR CAT A JET PACK

I bought our cat a jet pack,
which I think she liked a lot.
She strapped it on and instantly
she took off like a shot.

She zoomed around my bedroom,
then she blasted down the hall.
She ricocheted off every piece
of furniture and wall.

Our dog freaked out and ran away.
Our hamster squeaked and fled.
I even saw my sister hiding
underneath her bed.

Our cat is so fired up,
I almost hate to break the news:
She'll never catch our mouse;
I bought him rocket-powered shoes.

i HAVE TO WRITE A POEM

I have to write a poem,
but I really don't know how.
So maybe I'll just make a rhyme
with something dumb like "cow."

Okay, I'll write about a cow,
but that's so commonplace.
I think I'll have to make her be...
a cow from outer space!

My cow will need a helmet
and a space suit and a ship.
Of course, she'll keep a blaster
in the holster on her hip.

She'll hurtle through the galaxy
on meteoric flights
to battle monkey aliens
in huge karate fights.

She'll duel with laser sabers
while avoiding lava spray
to vanquish evil emperors
and always save the day.

I hope the teacher likes my tale,
"Amazing Astro Cow."
Yes, that's the poem I will write
as soon as I learn how.

MY CHICKEN'S ON THE INTERNET

My chicken's on the Internet.
She surfs the web all day.
I've tried to stop her browsing
but, so far, there's just no way.

She jumps up on the mouse,
and then she flaps around like mad
to click on every hyperlink
and every pop-up ad.

She plays all sorts of chicken games,
She messages her folks.
She watches chicken videos
and forwards chicken jokes.

She writes a blog for chickens
and she uploads chicken pics.
She visits chicken chat rooms
where she clucks about her chicks.

I wouldn't mind so much
except my keyboard's now a wreck.
She hasn't learned to type yet;
she can only hunt and peck.

SNAKE MISTAKE

One morning in my bedroom
I was startled by a snake,
so I picked him up and took him out
and threw him in the lake.

He returned a minute later,
meaning, no, he didn't drown,
so I put him on my bicycle
and rode him out of town.

It was hardly half an hour
till he turned up in my room,
so I packed him in a parcel,
and I shipped him to Khartoum.

When I found him back again
on the succeeding afternoon,
I went looking for a way that
I could blast him to the moon.

When I couldn't find a rocket
it was then I knew that, dang,
a snake is yours forever
once he eats your boomerang.

MY DOG IS NOT LIKE OTHER DOGS

My dog is not like other dogs.
He doesn't care to walk.
He doesn't bark; he doesn't howl.
He goes "Tick, tock. Tick, tock."

He beeps each day at half-past nine.
At noon he starts to chime.
I have a strong suspicion
that my dog can tell the time.

Another dog might run and play,
or smother me with licking,
but my dog just annoys me
with his beeping and his ticking.

Should you decide to buy a dog,
consider my remarks:
When looking for a "watch dog"
get yourself the kind that barks.

MY CAT GOES FLYING THROUGH THE AIR

My cat goes flying through the air
from over here to over there.
He lands and runs right back and then
goes flying through the air again.

I didn't used to see him fly,
like Superkitty, through the sky.
He used to only lie around
upon my bed or on the ground.

But now he's like an acrobat;
the coolest ever flying cat.
And how'd he get this great result?
He built himself a catapult.

17

A ROCK MAKES AN EXCELLENT PUPPY

A rock makes an excellent puppy.
They're practically almost the same.
Except that a puppy's rambunctious;
a rock is a little more tame.

It's true that a rock's not as hyper.
It may not chase after a ball.
And, often as not, when you call it,
it won't even hear you at all.

And maybe it doesn't roll over,
and isn't excited to play,
but rocks always sit when you tell them,
and rocks really know how to stay.

It may sleep a little bit longer.
It probably eats a bit less.
But rocks never pee on the carpet.
You won't have to pick up their mess.

So go ask your folks for a puppy,
and possibly that's what you'll get.
But, still, if you can't have a puppy,
a rock is a pretty good pet.

It doesn't annoy you with barking;
it quietly sits on a shelf.
A rock makes an excellent puppy.
That's what I keep telling myself.

DON'T EVER ASK A CENTIPEDE

Don't ever ask a centipede
to play a game of soccer.
Remember, he has fifty pairs
of sneakers in his locker.

He dribbles fifty soccer balls
with fifty pairs of shoes,
and kicks them all concurrently.
He doesn't often lose.

He's such a fierce competitor
that, if you ever meet,
at first you'll see his hundred legs
and then you'll see defeat.

POLAR BOWLiNG

It used to be that polar bears
went bowling, just for grins,
with snowballs for their bowling balls
and penguins as the pins.

The bears would have a blast
with all the snowballs that they threw.
The penguins weren't as happy;
that's the only time they flew.

So penguins all moved south and now
they're at the other pole.
Well, wouldn't you move far away
if bears used you to bowl?

HAS ANYONE SEEN MY CHAMELEON?

Has anyone seen my chameleon this morning?
He has to be hiding somewhere.
He asked me if we could play hide-and-go-seek
and then disappeared into thin air.

I've looked high and low in the yard and the house,
and it seems like he's nowhere around.
He's probably hiding right out in the open
but doesn't yet want to be found.

I'm guessing he looks like a leaf on a bush
or the back of a sofa or chair.
He could be disguised as a book or a bagel.
Regardless, I don't think it's fair.

If you come across my chameleon, please tell him
I give up. He beat me today.
He's clearly the champion at hiding so, next time,
it's my turn to pick what we play.

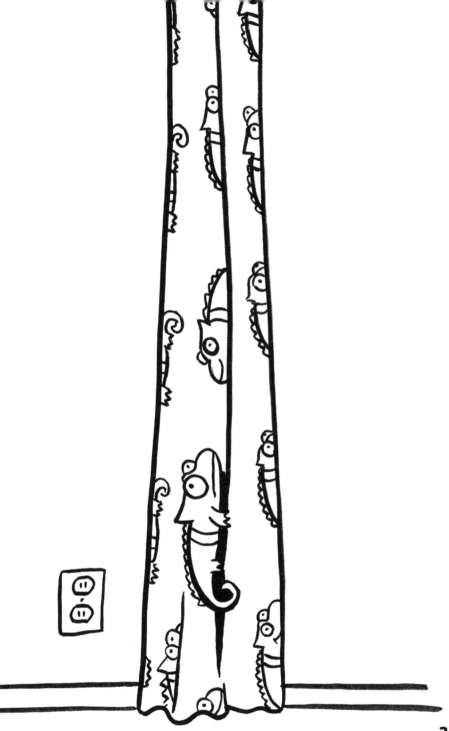

FERRET SOCCER

(to the tune of "Frère Jacques")

Ferret soccer!
Ferret soccer!
Come with me.
Let's go see.
I have heard that, mainly,
ferrets play insanely.
That sounds great!
I can't wait!

Ferret soccer.
Ferret soccer.
There's a kick,
hard and quick.
Aiming at the goalie,
but he's moving slowly.
Hit his snout.
Knocked him out!

Ferret soccer.
What a shocker.
Holy cow!
What's up now?
Took a new approach and
aimed it at the coach and
he's out cold.
That was bold!

Ferret soccer.
Off their rocker.
This is bad.
They've gone mad.
Sending balls a-flying.
Audience is crying.
Got us too.
Big boohoo.

Game is over.
Game is over.
Ferrets win.
See them grin.
That was such a thrill. Hey,
I can't wait until they
play again.
Let's go then.

i LiKE MY TRiANGULAR KiTTEN

I have a triangular kitten.
He has a triangular face.
He traipses triangular pathways
through any triangular space.

He plays with triangular cat toys.
He dreams of triangular fish.
He'd like to try angling for tuna
to fill his triangular dish.

Whenever his relatives visit,
he's pointedly pleasant and nice.
And, also, my kitten's unequaled
at catching triangular mice.

My kitten is clearly a cute one,
though often obtuse and oblique.
He hasn't a parallel out there;
he's plainly and flatly unique.

The point is we're right for each other.
He's simply the finest I've found.
I like my triangular kitten;
I think that I'll keep him around.

TODAY i TOUCHED THE BUFFALOBSTER

Today I touched the buffalobster
and the goldfishark,
the eagleopard, ocelotter,
and the weaselark.

I fed the frogorilla,
and I felt the reindeerat.
I prodded the piguana,
and I scratched the alpacat.

I gazed at the gazellephant.
I gawked at the gooseal.
I caught the cockroachimpanzeebra
and the bumblebeel.

I pet the parroturtle
and the pelicangaroo.
It's freaky, but it's fun here
at the Mutant Petting Zoo.

i BOUGHT A NEW TANK FOR MY GOLDFiSH

I bought a new tank for my goldfish.
They shot me right in the behind,
and then they drove over
my little dog, Rover.
I guess that I bought the wrong kind.

THE ELEPHANTS BOUNCED

The elephants bounced and propelled up the stairs.
The hippos did somersaults over their chairs.
The bison were bounding and so were the bears.
It was such a spectacular scene.

The cows were careening around in the den.
The rhinos went right through the ceiling, and then
my mom made me promise that never again
would I buy them a new trampoline.

iF YOU GiVE A MOUSE A MOTORCYCLE

If you give a mouse a motorcycle,
don't be too surprised
if he starts behaving strangely
once he knows he's motorized.

He may act a bit bizarrely.
He may dress a little weird.
He might buy a leather jacket
and then grow a honkin' beard.

When he straps a helmet on his head
and boots upon his feet,
then you'll see him pop a wheelie
and go racing down the street.

Pretty soon he'll find he's fond
of doing motorcycle tricks.
He'll be jumping over cars and trucks
and buses just for kicks.

He'll start working at the circus
where he'll take away your breath
as he rides with other rodents
in the flaming cage of death.

When he accidentally crashes,
he'll have no more fun and games;
just the screech of twisting metal
as his bike explodes in flames.

And without his motorcycle,
he'll be fired from his job.
He'll become depressed and lonely
and a sad and smelly slob.

And the only way to save him
from this misery and pain
is to buy another motorbike
so he can start again.

So remember this advice:
Don't even trust him with your keys.
If you need to give a mouse a gift,
it's best to stick with cheese.

ON TOP OF MOUNT EVEREST
(to the tune of "On Top of Old Smokey")

On top of Mount Everest,
all covered with snow,
a skiing gorilla
yelled, "Look out below!"

He skied down the mountain
at breathtaking speed
as everyone cheered at
his daredevil deed.

He skied down a glacier.
He flew off a jump
but bounced off a boulder
and tripped on a bump.

He staggered and stumbled.
He let out a yell.
He toppled and tumbled
and flipped as he fell.

So soon that gorilla
was covered with snow.
A big hairy snowball
that started to grow.

He rolled down the mountain.
He bounced and he flew,
then bumped into base camp;
his journey was through.

With skis sticking outward
like Popsicle sticks,
the people who saw him
applauded his tricks.

And when they unfroze him
and said what he'd done,
he got an idea and
a light bulb went on.

So now that gorilla
is a millionaire
for he had invented
the Popsicle there.

And now when he's skiing,
you won't see him crash.
Instead of Mount Everest,
he skis mountains of cash.

AN ORDINARY DAY

There's a dolphin on my doorstep.
It's an ordinary day.
He's delivering the paper
in his ordinary way.

There's a bison in my bathtub
singing ordinary songs,
and some hippos having ordinary
hippo sing-alongs.

In the pantry there's a penguin
painting ordinary scenes
of opossums in their ordinary
orange submarines.

There's an ordinary rhino
racing up and down the stairs,
chasing ordinary chimpanzees
and ordinary bears.

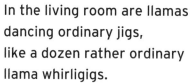

In the living room are llamas
dancing ordinary jigs,
like a dozen rather ordinary
llama whirligigs.

It's an ordinary day for me;
I promise you it's true.
And I hope you have a day that's
extra ordinary too.

THE DANCING BABOON OF DJIBOUTI

The Dancing Baboon of Djibouti
is known for his break-dancing skills.
He flips on his hips and his booty
from Boston to Beverly Hills.

He'll bounce from his back to his belly.
He'll hop on his hands and his chin.
He'll scissor from Dublin to Delhi,
then drop to his shoulders and spin.

He'll windmill from here to Helsinki.
He'll rocket from Reno to Rome,
then pike on the point of his pinky
and pretzel-hop into your home.

But if the Baboon of Djibouti
starts dancing inside your abode,
to run for your life is your duty,
for things are about to explode.

He'll smash all your glasses and vases.
He'll trash all your tables and chairs.
He'll pull all your books from their cases,
then throw your TV down the stairs.

He'll shatter your platters and pictures.
He'll crash through the windows and walls.
He'll fracture your bathtubs and fixtures.
He'll rip up the rugs in the halls.

It may be his footwork is funky,
but dancing just isn't enough,
for though he's a break-dancing monkey,
he's happier breaking your stuff.

WHEN PiGS FLY

I've heard it said that pigs will fly
and someday soon they'll rule the sky.
That may sound strange but, if it's right,
I don't suppose they'll fly a kite.
I'll bet, instead, they'll have to train
so they can learn to fly a plane,
or join the navy where they'll get
to learn to fly a fighter jet.

Or maybe they'll grow piggy wings,
or put on shoes with giant springs,
or fly in huge hot-air balloons,
or seaplanes with those big pontoons,
or biplanes like a flying ace,
or shuttles into outer space,
or rocket ships for trips to Mars,
or flying saucers to the stars.

However pigs decide to fly,
as long as they are way up high
and busy buzzing all around
instead of grunting on the ground,
I think it's safe to say I'll love
to see them soaring up above.
I'm sure I won't be shocked or shaken.
Still, I'll prob'ly miss the bacon.

MY HAMSTER HAS A SKATEBOARD

My hamster has a skateboard.
When he rides it, though, he falls.
He takes off like a maniac
and crashes into walls.

He screams, "Geronimo!"
and then goes crashing down the stairs.
He's good at knocking tables down
and slamming into chairs.

He'll slalom through the living room
and then you'll hear a "Splat!"
which means that he's collided with
my mother or the cat.

He plows right into cabinets
and smashes into doors;
I think he's wrecked on every bed
and every chest of drawers.

It's fun to watch him ride
because you're sure to hear a smash.
He doesn't skate so well but, boy,
he sure knows how to crash.

WHiLE LYiNG ON THE GRASS TODAY

While lying on the grass today
and staring at the sky,
I saw the strangest animals
in clouds that drifted by.

I saw a cloud that looked just like
an elephant on skis.
Another one reminded me
of dancing manatees.

I saw a duck on roller-skates
play jump rope with a snake,
and monkeys in a monster truck
drive right into a lake.

I watched a bungee-jumping cow,
and pigs on pogo sticks,
and beavers on their BMX bikes
doing gnarly tricks.

I spotted donkeys driving
demolition-derby cars
and spied a pride of lions
climbing giant monkey bars.

I even saw a surfing turkey
crash into a tree.
When you watch clouds go drifting by,
do you see what I see?

JUST A SLUG

Oh, I'm a slug,
a lowly bug,
who never does a thing,
although I'd like
to ride a bike
or maybe learn to sing.

And if I could,
I think I would
become a master spy.
Then go and get
a fighter jet
and really learn to fly.

I'd mountain climb.
I'd rap in rhyme.
I'd gain karate skills.
I'd bronco ride
and paraglide
and have some spills and thrills.

I'd take a trip
by rocket ship
to soar among the stars.
I'd travel free
past Mercury
and Jupiter and Mars.

The books I'd write!
The bulls I'd fight!
The places I would go!
If only I
were quick and spry
instead of sad and slow.

Alas, it seems,
despite my dreams,
I'll have to pull the plug
on all I ache
to undertake
for I am just a slug.

BANANA DAN

In the middle of the jungle,
in the tallest of the trees,
there's a monkey named Banana Dan
who's quaking on his knees.

It's a sad and sorry story,
but it's one that must be told,
as it used to be Banana Dan
was confident and bold.

He was once the monkey master
of a half a dozen sports.
When he played the game of basketball,
he used to rule the courts.

He could not be beat at racquetball
or bowling or lacrosse.
When it came to golf or volleyball,
Banana Dan was boss.

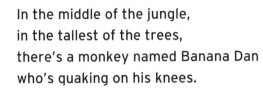

And whenever he would win a game,
bananas were the prize.
Yes, a hundred ripe bananas,
and you should have seen his eyes.

He would never take his winnings,
and he wouldn't even stay,
but instead Banana Dan would
always scream and run away.

Now he doesn't drive or dribble,
and he doesn't shoot and score,
and you'll never see him playing
in the jungle anymore.

He just sits up in his treetop
where he'll whimper and he'll pout,
as he has bananaphobia;
bananas freak him out.

GABBY'S BABY BEAGLE

Gabby bought a baby beagle
at the beagle baby store.
Gabby gave her beagle kibble,
but he begged for bagels more.

Gabby loved her baby beagle;
gladly Gabby gave him one,
but her beagle grabbed the bag and
gulped them down till there were none.

So she took her baby beagle
to the bagel baker's store,
where the beagle gobbled bagels,
bags of bagels by the score.

Gabby's beagle gorged on bagels,
bigger bagels than before,
till he'd gobbled every bagel
in the baker's bagel store.

Gulping bagels bulges baby
beagles' bellies really big.
Say good-bye to baby beagle;
Gabby's beagle's now a pig.

GERBiL, GERBiL, ON THE RUN

Gerbil, gerbil, on the run
in your wheel, that looks like fun.
You must be in awesome shape.
Are you trying to escape?

Is that why you dug a hole?
Where'd you get that vaulting pole?
That looks like my grappling hook.
Give me back that rope you took.

Tell me what that ladder's for.
Why's that hacksaw on the floor?
Are those cable cutters there?
Do I see a signal flare?

Crowbar, blowtorch, chain saw too?
What do you expect to do?
How'd you get that fuse to light?
Hey! That looks like dynamite!

Quick! Get out! It might explode!
Scram! Skedaddle! Hit the road!
Man, I'll miss you. You were fun.
Gerbil, gerbil, on the run.

SPEEDY SID

Speedy Sid, the racing squid,
has never lost a race.
The way he swims with all those limbs
ensures a lightning pace.

He's chased a flounder all around,
competed with an eel,
and raced a ray across the bay,
and even beat a seal.

And every place he's had a race,
you know he's been around,
for Speedy Sid, the racing squid,
leaves squid marks on the ground.

MY TURTLE IS THE SPORTING SORT

My turtle is the sporting sort.
His sports are all extreme.
He got so good at sleeping
that he joined the napping team.

He frequently competes
at moving slowly in the yard,
and, recently, he's got the hang
of staring very hard.

He races other turtles, seeing
who can come in last.
I hope you weren't expecting
that my turtle would be fast.

He's not too fond of motion,
so you'll never see him run.
He only plays the kinds of sports
that turtles think are fun.

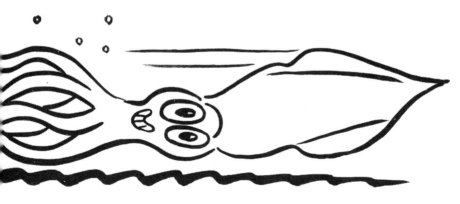

ABROCAT THE ACROBAT

I'm Abrocat the acrobat.
My shows are sure to please.
I practice my gymnastics act
on tightrope and trapeze.

I swing on things like ropes and rings.
I somersault and skip.
You'll be entranced to see me dance.
It's fair to say you'll flip.

I fly up there with feline flair,
and when my show's complete,
I end my act with skin intact
by landing on my feet.

I'm not at all afraid to fall
and never need a net.
The only things that frighten me
are dogs, and getting wet.

HiPPO SANDWiCH

If you're feeling fairly famished
and you really need to eat,
you should try a hippo sandwich;
it's a satisfying treat.

To prepare a hippo sandwich
with a minimum of fuss,
get a loaf of bread, a pickle,
and a hippopotamus.

If you do not like the flavor,
don't be worried, don't be flustered.
Just add hippopotamayonnaise
and hippopotamustard.

BELINDA BELL

Belinda Bell
could never tell
a crocodile
from a gator,
which made it so
she'll never know
which one of them
it was that ate her.

BEAVERS IN THE BATHROOM

There are beavers in the bathroom,
swimming circles in the tub,
where the beavers have decided
to convene their swimming club.

In their little beaver Speedos
and their beaver bathing caps,
they've been splashing rather happily
while practicing their laps.

They've been studying the butterfly,
the backstroke, and the crawl,
and it's obvious they like it,
and they're having quite a ball.

For we hear them all the time
though we don't see them anymore,
ever since they built a beaver dam
behind the bathroom door.

FORTY PURPLE PORPOISES

Forty purple porpoises
on forty silver sleds
went flying by with forty
flaming rockets on their heads.

64

As forty horses bungee jumped
from forty jumbo jets,
some forty mice on dirt bikes
raced with forty marmosets.

Then forty hippopotami
on forty snowmobiles
went screaming down a mountainside
with forty skiing seals.

And forty whales on skateboards
crashed in forty hockey rinks.
Yes, that's the dream I dreamed last night
while catching forty winks.

WHENEVER YAKS PLAY BASKETBALL

Whenever yaks play basketball,
it isn't any fun at all.
Their games are always such a snore.
They never shoot. They never score.

It seems they don't enjoy the sport.
They never run around the court.
Instead they simply settle back
and yak and yak and yak and yak.

MY CAMEL FiGHTS

My camel fights
with mighty knights.
It makes me feel distraught.
That's what I get;
I bought my pet
down at the Camelot.

FROM THE ANTS IN OUR PETUNIA BED

(to the tune of "The Marine's Hymn"
or "From the Halls of Montezuma")

From the ants in our petunia bed
to the earthworms in our lawn;
they've been practicing karate drills
every morning right at dawn.

All the beetles and the katydids
and the caterpillars too
have been learning judo, tae kwon do,
sumo wrestling, and kung fu.

They've been mastering the flying kick.
They've been breaking bricks and boards.
And I think they may have even learned
how to fight with ninja swords.

They've been marching all around the yard
to the sound of beating drums.
I would say they're nearly ready for
when the pest control guy comes.

TOBY THE SNOWBOARDING DOBERMAN

Toby the snowboarding Doberman pinscher
is king of the freestyling dogs.
Toby can turn and McTwist in the half-pipe
and ollie on boxes and logs.

No other Doberman's ever been known
who can slalom and slide on a rail.
Never before has a dog been discovered
to cartwheel and backflip and flail.

Toby can even leap into the air
and then spin through a 360 flip.
Sadly his talents are never enough
that they'll win him a championship.

True, he's the world's only snowboarding Doberman,
still, I expect you'll agree,
no one has ever been given a prize
when they're stopping to sniff every tree.

AT HAMSTER SAM'S RODEO

At Hamster Sam's Rodeo, tickets are free,
and, oh, the spectacular things that you'll see.

We're hamsters with cowboy boots, lassos, and chaps,
sombreros and saddles, bandanas and straps.

We even have hamsters for rodeo clowns,
with red rubber noses and painted-on frowns.

We spend our days racing and roping and riding
and wrestling and running and bucking and sliding.

It's nonstop excitement and guaranteed thrills,
with action and laughter and drama and spills.

And what's even better—on top of all that—
we haven't got horses; we ride on the cat.

MY PARROT DOESN'T CARE TO FLY

My parrot doesn't care to fly.
Although it sounds absurd,
he much prefers to sky dive.
He's a most peculiar bird.

You'll see him leap from airplanes
in his zip-up nylon suit,
with goggles and a helmet
and, of course, a parachute.

He plummets toward the earth and nearly
breaks the speed of sound,
then pulls the rip cord just in time
before he hits the ground.

He sky dives almost every day.
It leaves him feeling super.
And this is why he doesn't fly:
Yep, he's a parrotrooper.

WHEN RATTLESNAKES WEAR ROLLER-SKATES

When rattlesnakes wear roller-skates
it's quite a sight to see.
They figure skate in figure eights
enthusiastically.

They spin their partners round and round
and throw them through the air,
then swing them down around the ground
with fluidness and flair.

They slide and glide from side to side,
revolving all the while.
They skip and flip and zoom and zip
with elegance and style.

But skates for snakes are big mistakes
for, as they loop and leap,
they always land like pretzels in
a tied and twisted heap.

THE WEASEL AND THE WHALE

Have you ever heard the story of the weasel and
   the whale?
Well, I'll tell you, as it truly is an entertaining
   tale.
Let me introduce you, firstly, to the weasel, who,
   we note,
had a lifelong dream to water ski, but didn't own
   a boat.

No, he didn't have a speedboat or a rowboat or
a raft.
Not a kayak or containership or any kind of
craft.
Not a steamship or a sailboat or a dinghy or a
yacht.
Well, I think I've made my point, so I'll continue
with the plot.

He was walking down the beach one morning, sad to
be on land,
when he came upon a whining whale that whimpered
on the sand.
She was glad to see the weasel, and she blubbered,
"Help. I'm stuck."
Then the weasel, in his kindness, answered, "Let me
get my truck."

So the weasel hustled home and got his Chevy
  4X4,
and he backed it from the driveway, and he drove it
  to the shore,
where he gave the whale a gentle nudge and pushed
  her in the sea.
"Thank you! Thank you!" cried the whale, for she was
  happy to be free.

Then she told him, "Mr. Weasel, that was generous of
  you.
To repay you for your kindness, is there something
  I can do?"
It was then the weasel realized that maybe this
  could be
the solution to the problem of his dream to
  water ski.

So he told the whale his troubles and explained about
   his dream
and described how she could help him; how the two
   could be a team.
She was awfully glad to help him, and she instantly
   agreed,
so he got a pair of skis (because that's all he
   thought he'd need).

Then he brought them to the shoreline where he walked
   up to the whale,
and he stuck them on his feet and quickly grabbed her
   massive tail.
When the weasel hollered, "Go!" she gave it everything
   she'd got,
and she flipped her mighty tail and promptly took off
   like a shot.

But the weasel, sad to say, went flying wildly through
the air.
And it may be that he landed, but I couldn't tell you
where.
Though it's rumored that he made it, his demise is
widely feared,
And the only thing that's certain is he never
reappeared.

And he may be skiing somewhere, or it could be that
he's dead;
just that no one knows for certain is the best that
can be said.
So the moral of the story of the weasel and the
whale
is don't ever, ever, ever touch a whale upon her
tail.

GET ME OUT OF THE FiSH TANK
(to the tune of "Take Me Out to the Ball Game")

Get me out of the fish tank.
Get me out of this bowl.
I was just trying to catch the fish.
They looked tempting and awfully delish,
but I slipped and fell in the fish tank,
and now my future looks grim.
I just went to see and found out something:
Cats don't swim.

Won't you give me a hand here?
All I need is a lift.
Help and I promise I won't come back.
I'll go elsewhere when I need a snack,
for I've learned a valuable lesson;
I know it's not safe in here,
and the next time I want the fish I'll bring
scuba gear!

WE'RE SKYDIVING ELEPHANTS

We're skydiving elephants, bulging and bold.
We're dazzling and daring; a sight to behold.
We leap from our airplane at dizzying heights,
to soar through the sky on spectacular flights.

Our airborne maneuvers are one of a kind.
We spin in the air with our trunks intertwined.
We tuck and we tumble, we twist and we twirl.
We somersault freely, we wiggle and whirl.

We flip and we flutter while turning our tails,
unfurling our ears like magnificent sails.
We swivel and swim in a synchronized crawl
or swan dive in spirals as earthward we fall.

The onlookers gawk in an awestricken trance
to witness our wonderful aerial dance.
They clap at our kicks and rejoice at our rolls
and shriek as our landings leave walloping holes.

GORDON'S GARDEN

Gordon's garden's started growing
unexpected things,
and though it sounds unusual,
they all have beaks and wings.

His garden grew a hummingbird,
a heron, and a hawk,
a pelican, a parakeet,
a pigeon, and an auk.

It grew a cuckoo and a crow,
an ostrich and an owl,
an eagle and an egret,
and assorted other fowl.

A mockingbird, an oriole,
a chicken, and a duck.
It's fun to watch his garden grow
and chirp and flap and cluck.

It turns out growing gardens
full of birds is not so hard,
and Gordon got his crop
by planting birdseed in the yard.

CARA'S PARROT

Cara's parrot's rather rare.
He's such a quiet bird.
While other parrots talk a lot,
he never says a word.

It's not because he can't;
it's that he hasn't much to say.
Instead he's into bodybuilding,
lifting weights all day.

Although it sounds a little strange
and looks a bit bizarre,
he'll practice push-ups in his cage
and chin-ups on his bar.

He's gotten rather muscular
from lifting all day long.
It's safe to say you've never seen
a parrot quite so strong.

For Cara bought a parrot
of a somewhat different stripe.
It seems that Cara's parrot
is the strong and silent type.

MY DOG iS RUNNiNG FASTER

My dog is running faster
than he's ever run before
in a supersonic circle
in the middle of the floor.

He started somewhat slowly,
but he quickly gathered steam,
and continued gaining speed
until his spinning was extreme.

He's turned into a whirlwind,
like a funnel cloud of fog,
so it's hard to even focus on
my whirling-dervish dog.

He's like a small tornado
or a canine hurricane.
Why it doesn't make him dizzy,
I'm unable to explain.

I only know he has this
most unusual of traits,
and he loves to chase his tail around
while wearing roller-skates.

MONKEY DREAM

(to the tune of "The Battle Hymn of the Republic"
or "Glory, Glory, Hallelujah")

I dreamed that there were twenty monkeys bouncing on my bed.
They were jumping up and down and nearly landing on my head.
Then they started having pillow fights and throwing stuff instead.
I loved my dream that day!

CHORUS
Stuff went flying through the air then.
First a picture then a chair, then
all my socks and underwear then.
I loved my dream that day!

They ran around my bedroom throwing basketballs and bats.
They had toppled all my trophies. They were tossing all my hats.
It was obvious those monkeys were a bunch of little brats.
I'm not sure what to say!

CHORUS
Books went flying out the door, and
clothes were pulled from every drawer, and
junk had covered up the floor, and
I wished they'd go away!

I woke to find my bedroom a complete and total mess.
It was utterly in shambles and a state of some distress.
Then I knew my dream was just a dream for, sadly, I confess,
it always looks this way!

KiTTEN FiGHT

My cat had kittens recently.
Her litter's awfully cute.
I like to watch them wrestling.
I think it's such a hoot.

Her litter likes to roll around.
They like to scratch and bite.
They kick each other constantly.
It's fun to watch them fight.

But, even so, I'll pick them up
and put them all to bed
the minute they start punching
one another in the head.

I'm not concerned her kittens
couldn't take a couple knocks.
It's just that I don't like to watch
her kitty litter box.

i SAW A SLOTH PLAY SOCCER

I saw a sloth play soccer
with a tortoise and a snail.
They were all enthusiastic
and determined to prevail.

They were positively passionate
and truly in the groove,
and by watching very closely,
I could almost see them move.

AN ELEPHANT FOLLOWED ME HOME

An elephant followed me home today
after waiting outside my class.
He patiently puttered around all day
playing hopscotch and munching grass.

He followed me out to the parking lot
and then rode with me on the bus.
He squeezed in the back near my normal spot
while the other kids stared at us.

He came in my house like a dog or cat
after smashing in through the door.
At dinner he pulled up a chair and sat
and then fell through the kitchen floor.

I'm trying to sleep, but it's really tough
with an elephant in my bed.
He's heavy and huge, and his skin is rough,
and his trunk is across my head.

So though it may not seem relevant,
please remember to heed this warning:
Don't ever give nuts to an elephant
if he follows you in the morning.

TRACK 42

iF YOU HAPPEN TO HOP

If you happen to hop on a boa constrictor,
you'll find it's a fabulous ride,
just as long as you're strong
and can hop on the top,
for it's never as fun from inside.

i HAVE AN AMOEBA

I have an amoeba I keep as a pet.
Today is his birthday; I didn't forget.
I baked him a cake so incredibly small,
a microscope's needed to see it at all.

This miniscule morsel's so meager and scant,
it wouldn't suffice as a snack for an ant.
There isn't a flea this confection would feed;
this particle pastry is paltry indeed.

It's infinitesimal, barely a speck.
I managed to frost it with less than a fleck.
I topped it with candles of miniature size,
to give my amoeba his birthday surprise.

At last it was ready; the cake was all set,
and just the right size for my single-celled pet.
The candles were lit. It was perfectly frosted.
I set the cake down, and I instantly lost it.

ACKNOWLEDGMENTS

To the readers of poetry4kids.com, you have my deepest thanks for taking the time to read and rate the poems on the website. Your ratings helped select the poems in this crazy collection. Thank you Madison, Max, and Ann for your support and the occasional unintentional idea. To my editor, Daniel Ehrenhaft, it was a joy to work with you on this book. To Dominique, Rebecca, Kelly, Kristin, and Paul, and everyone else at Sourcebooks, thank you for helping to make this book the magnificent piece of folderol it is. To Elbert, my invisible long-eared Norwegian spider monkey, thank you for the jet pack, the crash helmet, and all of the cheese, without which I could not have written this book. And finally, thank you to all of the teachers, librarians, and parents who make childhood fun by sharing poetry with your kids.

iNDEX

ABOUT THE AUTHOR

Kenn Nesbitt is possibly the funniest and most sought-after children's poet writing today. As a child he once got lost during a field trip to the zoo and was raised by animals who taught him their secret ways. He used that knowledge to create this book, every word of which is true. Really. Okay, not really. He just wanted to see if you would read this page. When he is not writing, podcasting, or updating his website, poetry4kids .com, Kenn is visiting schools and libraries, sharing his wacky brand of humor with kids around the world.

ABOUT THE ILLUSTRATOR

Ethan Long is a children's book author and illustrator whose titles include the extremely popular *Tickle the Duck!* and the hilarious sequel *Stop Kissing Me!* He was taught how to draw by a wild boar in the deep woods of Pennsylvania. He started out learning with his feet, but eventually his hands grew in and he made the switch. Now look at him. He's a professional artist and loving life. It's a dream come true. "True" being the drawing and the deep woods of Pennsylvania part. Not the part about the wild boar and drawing with his feet. Nor the part about his hands growing in. That's kind of sick.

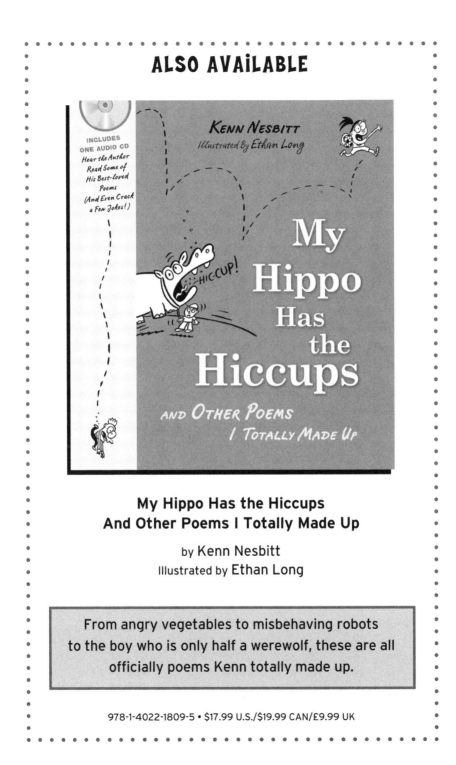